Nine bright pennies don't seem like a lot.

But that's all Maggie had,
and here's what she got:

She hurried off to the candy store...

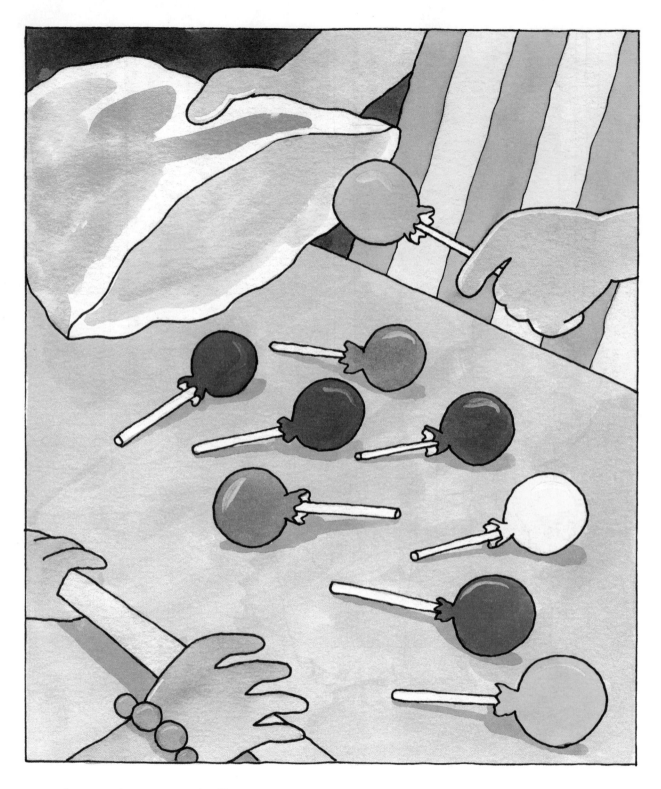

bought nine lollipops—
no less, no more.

Maggie traded the candy to her cousin Boris...

and walked away with nine Stegosauruses.

Maggie traded those dinos to her
best friend June...

and strolled away with nine balloons.

She traded the balloons to Polly Parker...

and headed home with nine colored markers.

Maggie sold the markers to her brother Reese,
who bought them all for a penny apiece.

Nine bright pennies
don't seem like a lot.

But they're exactly enough
when you're thirsty and hot!

Can you find...

nine pennies, nine dinos, nine marbles of blue,
nine toy cars, nine markers, nine cookies, too?

What other sets of nine can you find?

Hooray for Nine!

Let's clap nine times
and touch the ground.
Let's jump nine times
and spin around.
Let's stomp nine times
and cheer and shout
for a wonderful number
we can't live without:
 NINE!